MW01291042

TABLE OF CONTEN s

DISCLAIMER AND TERMS OF USE AGREEMENT:

Introduction – There Are Two Sides to Every Argument

Chapter 1 - Laying A Proper Foundation

Chapter 2 – Inductive Reasoning

Chapter 3 – Deductive Reasoning

Chapter 4 – Intellectual versus Emotional Decisions

Chapter 5 – Why We Must Decide

Chapter 6 – Summing It All Up

I Have a Special Gift for My Readers

Meet the Author

How To Figure Things Out
Inductive Reasoning versus Deductive Reasoning
©Copyright 2014 by Dr. Treat Preston

DISCLAIMER AND TERMS OF USE AGREEMENT:

(Please Read This Before Using This Book)

This information is for educational and informational purposes only. The content is not intended to be a substitute for any professional advice, diagnosis, or treatment.

The authors and publisher of this book and the accompanying materials have used their best efforts in preparing this book.

The authors and publisher make no representation or warranties with respect to the accuracy, applicability, fitness, or completeness of the contents of this book. The information contained in this book is strictly for educational purposes. Therefore, if you wish to apply ideas contained in this book, you are taking full responsibility for your actions.

The authors and publisher disclaim any warranties (express or implied), merchantability, or fitness for any particular purpose. The author and publisher shall in no event be held liable to any party for any direct, indirect, punitive, special, incidental or other consequential damages arising directly or indirectly from any use of this material, which is provided "as is", and without warranties. As always, the advice of a competent legal, tax, accounting, medical or other professional should be sought where applicable.

The authors and publisher do not warrant the performance, effectiveness or applicability of any sites listed or linked to in this book. All links are for information purposes only and are not warranted for content, accuracy or any other implied or explicit purpose. No part of this may be copied, or changed in any format, or used in any way other than what is outlined within this course under any circumstances. Violators will be prosecuted.

This book is © Copyrighted by ePubWealth.com.

Introduction – There Are Two Sides to Every Argument

	Deductive Reasoning	Inductive Reasoning
Premises	Stated as facts or general principles ("It is warm in the summer in Spain.")	Based on observations of specific cases ("All crows Knut and his wife have seen are black.")
Conclusion	Conclusion is more special than the information the premises provide. It is reached directly by applying logical rules to the premises.	Conclusion is more general than the information the premises provide. It is reached by generalizing the premises' information.
Validity	If the premises are true, the conclusion must be true.	If the premises are true, the conclusion is probably true.
Usage	More difficult to use (mainly in logical problems). One needs facts which are definitely true.	Used often in everyday life (fast and easy). Evidence is used instead of proved facts.

This will quickly become a very unusual book to read. Unfortunately, deductive reasoning versus inductive reasoning is not something that is taught in the schools today and it is a shame.

Read the chart above to see the differences between deductive reasoning and inductive reasoning.

Learning to figure things out for yourself is actually fun but more importantly it is a learned experience that trains the human mind to see both sides of an argument and then allows the person to make a choice but a choice based on facts rather than feelings, hence you make better choices!!!

As I do in all of my "human mind" books, Chapter 1 is about the "Mechanism of the Human Mind" and how the mind functions as well as how each gender employs their respective psyches. It is equally important to learn and understand how your mind works and why you do the things you do. Once you have learned about your mind, the contents of this book will quickly fall in place.

Below is a series of article that I feel will introduce you to the topic of "Deductive and Inductive Arguments". After you read the articles I will comment on them and further the learning cycle. The items in bold are mine and are items I need you to remember.

*****

Internet Encyclopedia of Philosophy
A Peer-Reviewed Academic Resource

Deductive and Inductive Arguments
http://www.iep.utm.edu/ded-ind/

A *deductive argument* is an argument that is intended by the arguer to be (deductively) *valid*, that is, to provide a *guarantee* of the truth of the conclusion provided that the argument's premises (assumptions) are true. This point can be expressed also by saying that, in a deductive argument, the premises are intended to provide such strong support for the conclusion that, if the premises are true, then it would be *impossible* for the conclusion to be false. An argument in which the premises do succeed in guaranteeing the conclusion is called a (deductively) valid argument. If a valid argument has true conclusions, then the argument is said to be *sound*.

Here is a valid deductive argument: It's sunny in Singapore. If it's sunny in Singapore, he won't be carrying an umbrella. So, he won't be carrying an umbrella.

Here is a mildly strong inductive argument: Every time I've walked by that dog, he hasn't tried to bite me. So, the next time I walk by that dog he won't try to bite me.

An *inductive argument* is an argument that is intended by the arguer merely to establish or increase the probability of its conclusion. In an inductive argument, the premises are intended only to be so strong that, if they were true, then it would be *unlikely* that the conclusion is false. There is no standard term for a successful inductive argument. But its success or strength is a matter of degree, unlike with deductive arguments. A deductive argument is valid or else invalid.

The difference between the two kinds of arguments does not lie solely in the words used; it comes from the relationship the author or expositor of the argument takes there to be between the premises and the conclusion. **If the author of the argument believes that the truth of the premises *definitely establishes* the truth of the conclusion (due to definition, logical entailment, logical structure, or mathematical necessity), then the argument is *deductive*. If the author of the argument does not think that the truth of the premises definitely establishes the truth of the conclusion, but nonetheless believes that their truth provides good reason to believe the conclusion true, then the argument is *inductive*.**

Some analysts prefer to distinguish inductive arguments from conductive arguments; the latter are arguments giving explicit reasons for and against a conclusion, and requiring the evaluator of the argument to weigh these considerations, i.e., to consider the pros and cons. This article considers conductive arguments to be a kind of inductive argument.

The noun "deduction" refers to the process of advancing or establishing a deductive argument, or going through a process of reasoning that can be reconstructed as a deductive argument. "Induction" refers to the process of advancing an inductive argument, or making use of reasoning that can be reconstructed as an inductive argument.

Because deductive arguments are those in which the truth of the conclusion is thought to be completely *guaranteed* and not just *made probable* by the truth of the premises, if the argument is a sound one, then the truth of the conclusion is said to be "contained within" the truth of the premises; that is, the conclusion does not go beyond what the truth of the premises implicitly requires. **For this reason, deductive arguments are usually limited to inferences that follow from definitions, mathematics and rules of formal logic.** Here is a deductive argument:

John is ill. If John is ill, then he won't be able to attend our meeting today. Therefore, John won't be able to attend our meeting today.

That argument is valid due to its logical structure. If 'ill' were replaced with 'happy', the argument would still be valid because it would retain its special logical structure (called *modus ponens*). Here is the form of any argument having the structure of modus ponens:

P

If P then Q

So, Q

The capital letters stand for declarative sentences, or statements, or propositions. The investigation of these logical forms is called Propositional Logic:

http://www.iep.utm.edu/prop-log/

The question of whether all, or merely most, valid deductive arguments are valid because of their structure is still controversial in the field of the philosophy of logic, but that question will not be explored further in this article.

Inductive arguments can take very wide ranging forms. Inductive arguments might conclude with some claim about a group based only on information from a sample of that group. Other inductive arguments draw conclusions by appeal to evidence or authority or causal relationships. Here is a somewhat strong inductive argument based on authority:

The police said John committed the murder. So, John committed the murder.

Here is an inductive argument based on evidence:

The witness said John committed the murder. So, John committed the murder.

Here is a stronger inductive argument based on better evidence:

Two independent witnesses claimed John committed the murder. John's fingerprints are the only ones on the murder weapon. John confessed to the crime. So, John committed the murder.

This last argument is no doubt good enough for a jury to convict John, but none of these three arguments about John committing the murder is strong enough to be called valid. At least it is not valid in the technical sense of 'deductively valid'. However, some lawyers will tell their juries that these are valid arguments, so we critical thinkers need to be on the alert as to how people around us are using the term.

It is worth noting that some dictionaries and texts improperly define "deduction" as *reasoning from the general to specific* and define "induction" as *reasoning from the specific to the general*. These definitions are outdated and inaccurate. For example, according to the more modern definitions given above, the following argument from the specific to general is deductive, not inductive, because the truth of the premises *guarantees* the truth of the conclusion:

The members of the Williams family are Susan, Nathan and Alexander.

Susan wears glasses.
Nathan wears glasses.
Alexander wears glasses.

Therefore, *all* members of the Williams family wear glasses.

Moreover, the following argument, even though it reasons from the general to specific, is inductive:

It has snowed in Massachusetts *every* December in recorded history.

Therefore, it will snow in Massachusetts this coming December.

It is worth noting that the proof technique used in mathematics called "mathematical induction", is deductive and not inductive. Proofs that make use of mathematical induction typically take the following form:

Property P is true of the number 0.
For all natural numbers n, if P holds of n then P also holds of $n + 1$.
Therefore, P is true of *all* natural numbers.

When such a proof is given by a mathematician, it is thought that if the premises are true, then the conclusion follows necessarily. Therefore, such an argument is deductive by contemporary standards.

Because the difference between inductive and deductive arguments involves the strength of evidence which the author *believes* the premises to provide for the conclusion, inductive and deductive arguments differ with regard to the standards of evaluation that are applicable to them. The difference does not have to do with the content or subject matter of the argument. Indeed, the same utterance may be used to present either a deductive or an inductive argument, depending on the intentions of the person advancing it. Consider as an example.

Dom Perignon is champagne, so it must be made in France.

It might be clear from context that the speaker believes that having been made in the Champagne area of France is part of the defining feature of "champagne" and so the conclusion follows from the premise by definition. If it is the intention of the speaker that the evidence is of this sort, then the argument is deductive. However, it may be that no such thought is in the speaker's mind. He or she may merely believe that nearly all champagne is made in France, and may be reasoning probabilistically. If this is his or her intention, then the argument is inductive.

It is also worth noting that, at its core, the distinction between deductive and inductive has to do with the strength of the justification that the author or expositor of the argument *intends* that the premises provide for the conclusion. If the argument is logically fallacious, it may be that the premises *actually* do not provide justification of that strength or even any justification at all. Consider the following argument:

All odd numbers are integers.
All even numbers are integers.
Therefore, all odd numbers are even numbers.

This argument is logically fallacious because it is invalid. In actuality, the premises provide *no support whatever* for the conclusion. However, if this argument were ever seriously advanced, we must assume that the author would *believe* that the truth of the premises guarantees the truth of the conclusion. Therefore, this argument is still deductive. **A bad deductive argument is not an inductive argument.**

*****

You may need to read the articles multiple times for the differences to sink in. As you do, you will find that the differences are not as difficult as they first seem.

The crux of both deductive and inductive reasoning is a system of reasoning that allows you to figure things out and now I am going to show you how.

Most people today rely on feelings rather than facts when they make a decision or attempt to figure things out. I am going to demonstrate why this is wrong.

Are you ready? Let's get at it…

Chapter 1 - Laying A Proper Foundation

In all of my "human mind" series of books, I will provide the following discourse on the Human Mind in order to lay a proper foundation to what I am about to teach.

The Mechanism of the Human Mind

Which Comes First - the Body or the Mind?

(the most important concept in all of talk therapy)

Understanding the Body - Mind Connection

For thousands of years, we have known there is a body – mind connection. Until now though, we have not known what this connection is. What it it? Time. The body and the mind each have their own sense of time. Their own clocks so to speak. Therapy works only when these two clocks are in sync.

Body First Person   Body – Mind in sync   Mind First Person

time

Prior to the fall of man into sin as described in the Garden of Eden, man's spirit was hooked to God's infinite spirit. There was no death because God's spirit is infinite. Man is the only animal on earth that shares the eternality nature of God. The subject of eternal life has been a heated topic of man from the beginning of our existence.

In Greek mythology, there's a story about a mortal youth named Tithonus. Aurora, the goddess of dawn, fell in love with the boy and when Zeus, the king of the gods, promised to grant Aurora any gift she chose for her lover, she asked that Tithonus might live forever. But, in her haste she forgot to ask for eternal youth, so when Zeus granted her request, Tithonus was doomed to an eternity of perpetual aging as a grouchy old man... forever.

In the movie "Highlander," Angus McLeod was born in 1518 as an immortal being. He could not die and to me, the best part of the movie was the depiction of this immortal's agony here on earth as he watched everything he loved die forcing him to begin his life over and over again. He saw all of the ugliness, which man had caused over four centuries. He witnessed the Spanish Inquisition, Waterloo, the atrocities of the Third Reich, and more. He saw the slavery and bigotry of the eighteenth century, the slaughter of the Native American tribes after the Civil War. This man's life was a living Hell!

There is a very big difference between the ways our feeble minds picture eternal life versus God's idea of eternal life. Our understanding comes from Quantum Physics and is limited within the Time-Space Continuum.

Life is your spirit, but the soul of man has usurped the spirit's position and psychology is now forced to define "how" we live our lives based on the animating force of the soul instead of the spirit. As I said previously, the soul has usurped the spirit's place as our animating force. Let's discuss this now.

- ❖ **Body First Person** - When the body becomes our life, we live as animals.
- ❖ **Body-Mind In Sync** - When the soul becomes our life, we live as rebels and fugitives in a life of desires, emotions, and will (consuming entities). This is the position of mankind today!
- ❖ **Mind First Person** - But when we come to live our life in the mind/spirit and by the spirit, though we still use our soul's faculties just as we do our physical faculties, they are now the servants of the spirit.

If you live as a consuming entity, you will always lose. In other words, to get, you must give - you must sacrifice! Have you ever wondered why you have so many anxieties, phobias, worries and fears? The reality of this world is evil. So what is reality? I will tell you. This is reality:

"Life without war is impossible either in nature or in grace. The basis of physical, mental, moral and spiritual life is antagonism. Health is the balance between physical life and external nature, and it is maintained only by sufficient vitality on the inside against things on the outside. Everything outside my physical life is designed to put me to death. Things, which keep me going when I

17

am alive, disintegrate me when I am dead. If I have enough fighting power, I produce the balance of health.

The same is true of mental life. If I want to maintain a vigorous mental life, I have to fight, and in that way the mental balance called thought is produced. Morally it is the same. Everything that does not partake of the nature of virtue is the enemy of virtue in me, and it depends on what moral caliber I have whether I overcome and produce virtue (GOOD CHARACTER). Immediately I fight, I am moral in that particular. No man is virtuous because he cannot help it; virtue (character) is acquired.

❖ Psychology only studies the observable aspects of the mind and discounts the unseen or intangible aspects of the human mind.
❖ Behavioral science attempts to study the intangible aspects of the human mind…why you do the things you do and more importantly why you don't do what you should do.
❖ There is no such thing as commercial psychology versus personal psychology. The mind uses the same mechanism to evaluate all types of relationships.
❖ Everything we do revolves around relationships. We relate to our environment, our friends, family, co-workers, other people and even our pets. We are social animals.

The Mechanism of the Human Mind

Belief Systems + Thought + Delight = Action/Behavior/Conduct

Conscious Mind

5-senses:
Sight
Hearing
Taste
Touch
Smell
ESP (women only)

Subconscious Mind

Intellect:
Experiential
Empirical

DEW:
Desires, Emotions and Will

The Human Psyche Differences Between Genders

The female psyche operates on emotional, spiritual, physical and intellectual planes
The male psyche operates only on the intellectual and physical planes.

Here is an exercise you might find weird but it demonstrates the power of the human mind.

Fi yuo cna raed tihs, yuo hvae a sgtrane mnid too. Cna yuo raed tihs? Olny 55 plepoe out of 100 can. I cdnuolt blveiee taht I cluod aulaclty uesdnatnrd waht I was rdanieg. The phaonmneal pweor of the hmuan

mnid, aoccdrnig to a rscheearch at Cmabrigde Uinervtisy, it dseno't mtaetr in waht oerdr the ltteres in a wrod are, the olny iproamtnt tihng is taht the frsit and lsat ltteer be in the rghit pclae. The rset can be a taotl mses and you can sitll raed it whotuit a pboerlm. Tihs is bcuseae the huamn mnid deos not raed ervey lteter by istlef, but the wrod as a wlohe. Azanmig huh? Yaeh and I awlyas tghuhot slpeling was ipmorantt!

You might have found it somewhat unusual that you could probably read the jumbled mess above. Actually over half the people that see this exercise can decipher the words at the same speed of reading as if the words were not jumbled.

It is important to note that the human mind thinks in packages...concepts rather than individual ideas.

Your eyes see each letter but the mind looks at the whole word instead. As you read, the mind looks at the first and last letter only. Remember this; the mind sees the beginning and end. We will talk about this later...

If you were to listen to an orchestra, your ear listens to every note from every instrument but a trained ear can actually pick out individual instruments from the whole sound as the mind hears the whole symphony.

How does this apply to you?

Learning to observe means going beyond the mind's natural ability to only read the first and last letters of a word!

It is training the mind to see all the letters, not just the eye but the mind!

Truisms About the Human Mind

* Pain vs. Pleasure – people are more motivated to avoid pain than seek pleasure.
* A person that is suffering depression will seek relief (notice I didn't say cure) before they seek happiness.
* The human mind cannot tell the difference between fantasy and reality.
* The human mind gravitates to the desires, emotions and will of its psyche. People crave entertainment so fantasy dominates their existences.
* The human mind is easily distracted! You can either be the cause of these distractions or other stimuli will be the cause but rest assured people WILL BE distracted because the human mind is gullible.

The human mind responds quickly to these three forms of stimuli

* Sex
* Humor
* FEAR

But the greatest of them all is FEAR!

BTW – on the positive side we have faith, hope, love, but the greatest of these *is* LOVE.

Fear usually takes the form of what is called "Scarcity Thought"

You are afraid that someone will have what you feel belongs to you or that others will have more "stuff" than you.

❖ The subconscious mind is often referred to as the "heart," and is the control mechanism the body uses to store our beliefs.

❖ **These beliefs are stored as pictures in our "hearts" and create frequencies in our bodies.**

❖ We know that the optimum human frequency is a little below 7.83 hertz. To drop below this frequency brings on the onslaught of disease. To rise above it a person demonstrates psychic abilities.

❖ Harmful beliefs that cause unhealthy frequencies are the source of almost all problems - physical, mental, emotional.

❖ The subconscious mind creates a belief system, which we call "pictures of the heart."

❖ These pictures involve either visions, or dreams/fantasies.

❖ Science has discovered that the subconscious mind cannot distinguish between fantasy and reality.

*The subject of all dreams is the dreamer.
*Dreams are born in our desires, emotions and will.
*Dreamers believe in a belief system, which is fantasy.
*A life lived within a fantasy creates a feeling of self-centeredness, hopelessness and despair.   In dreams everything is perfect.
*The subject of a vision is not the visionary but the world.
*Visions are born in the intellect.
*Visions are pictures of the future that have already been experienced in the heart of those who give it birth.
*Visionaries sacrifice themselves for the good of mankind.
*Visions have a moral quality that transcends the self-centered nature of dreams.
*By its very nature a vision launches a mission, a "cause-that-inspires."
*Visions create a sense of belonging.

❖ We act upon visions and/or dreams, using thought.
❖ Thought employs the intellect, in the case of visions, or the desires, emotions and the will, in the case of dreams.
❖ Intellectual thought relies on wisdom; emotional thought relies on the pursuit of pleasure, comfort and delight.
❖ Dreamers live within a facade; they create a false sense of worth using imaginary situations.

- ❖ Visionaries live within reality; they create change, within a framework of restraint, and intellectual thought.
- ❖ The world is made up of OPPOSITES, which is usually the corrupted version of the original. We have good and evil. We have love and lust!
- ❖ EVERYTHING YOU DO IS BECAUSE OF LOVE OR LUST. Learn to love because there are no crimes beyond forgiveness.

*Love is born in the intellect; lust is born in the DEW!
*Love is vision; lust is fantasy.
*Love restrains & sacrifices; lust is selfish
*Love is being one with someone or something
*Lust is being with someone or something.
*Visionaries love; dreamers lust!
*Visionaries do what is required; dreamers just do their best!

WHEN THERE IS NO HOPE OF LOVE DO WE ABANDON OURSELVES TO LUST?

Yes we do!

Pictures of the heart are your belief system.

- ❖ We animate these pictures into either fantasies, or visions.
- ❖ People do not appear to see the difference between the matter part of an organism and the life part, which animates it.

- We seem to think that the organism itself is life. In other words, it is not our outward appearance that is our life, but our inward existence.
- Life is what goes into the body. Death is what comes out.
- A person who lies is not a liar because he tells a lie. The lie is the manifested behavior of some subconscious belief system. The lie only demonstrates that the person is a liar…it is the effect.
- Except for love, the power of words inspired by a vision or fantasy is the most potent human force.

"Do you want to have or do you want to be?"

*For a dreamer: "Seeing is believing!"
*But they only see imaginary things that are not real!!
*This is why "The Secret" is WRONG!
*Say it and claim it is WRONG!
*Blab it and grab it IS WRONG!
*See it and be it IS WRONG!
Dreamers practice companionship – To be with someone or something!

VERY IMPORTANT:

1. Dreamers covet the object of their temptation, BUT they covet the temptation more so than the object itself because the temptation is the idol of their fantasy.
2. If there is a conflict between the conscious and subconscious mind, the subconscious mind always wins…ALWAYS!

25

3. All reaction occurs in the conscious mind; all interaction occurs in the subconscious mind. Fear is a "REACTION" to losing control.

For a visionary: "Believing is seeing!"

There are no SECRETS; there are only challenges to be conquered!

THIS IS NOT A SECRET: Putting a photo of a Ferrari on your refrigerator and seeing yourself driving it by employing the so-called law of attraction is pure BUPKES!!! Why? Because this is all occurring in the conscious mind and beliefs reside in the subconscious mind. How do you transfer something from the conscious mind to the subconscious mind and make it a belief system?

A Ferrari is the object of your temptation but what you covet most is the temptation of owning a Ferrari because the temptation is the idol of your fantasy.

It is all about ATTENTION & ACCEPTANCE!!!!! I have a $100 bill in my hand and I am willing to give it to you. But if you don't ACCEPT it then it is still in my hand. BELIEF SYSTEMS ARE CREATED BY ATTENTION & ACCEPTANCE!

John 1:12 But as many as received him, to them gave he **the right** to become children of God, *even* to them that believe on his name

Human things must be known to be loved; but divine things must be loved to be known.

BELIEVING IS SEEING!

Let's talk about goals...which of the following goals are good goals?

❖ To want to get married and have a wonderful, happy, loving marriage?
❖ To want to have children who are happy, successful, and loving?
❖ To have a successful, fulfilling and rewarding career?
❖ Is it a good goal to want to have fun, bonded, loving, and meaningful relationships with other people?

Which of the listed goals are good goals? None of them!

You should never have anything for a goal that is not 100% under your control, AND each and every goal should be motivated by love.

Almost all goals that we have in our life are wrong.

Everything that we do, we do because of a goal we have.

When we get up in the morning, it's because of some goal that we have; we are hungry for breakfast, or we need to go to work.

If we go to the grocery store, it's because of some goal we have. If we are kind to people, it's because of some goal that we have.

Now we don't always know what they are, because a lot of these are subconscious goals.

The goals we have are the reasons for everything we do. But, do all of your goals involve only YOU?

Of course not!

And when the other person, or persons, in your goal do not perform, or act the way you want them to, then we become anxious and stressed.

When our goals get blocked, it creates anger, anxiety, and frustration. If we only have good goals, we will not experience anger or anxiety.

That's how you know, if you are living a wrongful goal. If the result is anger and frustration because your control was blocked and blocking your goal, then you had a wrongful goal. It may have been a fine and noble desire, but a wrongful goal.

Filters

We live in a society of consumerism and entertainment. In my previous books I have spoken reams about this subject. Instant gratification is paramount and today's technology delivers information and other stimuli in bucketfuls to the human mind. We have already spoken about filters that the human mind employs to weed out what it determines to be irrelevant. This "irrelevancy" is different in every individual and many times is programmed into our minds subconsciously or without us knowing it. We have also spoken about the causes of these various filters such as environment, maturity, upbringing, culture, etc.

The one essential common element of all filters is that they are all ATTENTION diverters. We have spoken about attention earlier; what is very interesting is that filters are generally viewed as bad when some are really very good.

I had a friend who lives in Chicago fall on hard times and needed assistance. When I got to him he was living in a cheap hotel and had a room so small when you put the key in the door you broke the *window (I slay me)*. His room was about 50 feet from the Loop (the overhead train that circles around Chicago). The noise was deafening when the train went by, and it went by often, but my friend had filtered it out. Amazing, but when you thing about it, my friend really does hear the train but yet he pays no attention to it, so in actuality, it is like he doesn't hear it at all! So filters divert attention, and take away our focus; so let's talk about focus.

The Incredible Power of Focus
One of the more important points I have made has been the idea that you really do create your own life and your own reality. I know this idea has become a kind of personal growth cliché that many of us have heard over and over for years. Many people, after continuing to experience the same old ups and downs and personal dramas over many years, get to the point where they dismiss this idea as charming but useless -- or just plain

wrong. "If I'm creating this, then I'm certainly not doing it on purpose," they say. "It sure seems like this is HAPPENING to me, rather than that I'm creating it." They just assume that it's all BS because "this and this and this and this are going on for me, and I have no control over it, and anyone who thinks I'm creating this doesn't understand what I'm going through." Essentially, they are resigning themselves to becoming a victim of circumstances.

We live in a universe of infinite complexity and many forces -- way too many to keep track of -- operate on us. Yes, it is true that we are NOT in control of everything that happens, because we are not in control of most of those infinite other parts of the universe. In fact, the only thing you have total and complete control over is...YOUR OWN MIND. That is, if you learn how to exercise it.

Luckily, this one thing -- your mind -- that you do have control over gives you tremendous power. By exercising control over your mind, you can get the rest of those infinite other parts of the universe to begin to march in formation.

The person who says, "If I'm creating this, it certainly isn't on purpose," is right. They are not creating what is happening to them "on purpose." Who would purposely create failure, or bad relationships, or any other kind of suffering? You can only do something that is not good for you that is harmful to you, if you do it subconsciously. This means if you are creating something you don't want, you must be doing so subconsciously.

Your mind is running on automatic pilot, based on "software" (subconscious programming) installed when you were too young to know any better, by parents, teachers, friends, the media, and other experiences and influences. The key is to become more conscious, more aware...to get yourself off automatic pilot. Once you do this, you stop creating all the dramas and other garbage you don't want in your life.

How do you do this? One way is by remembering and using a very important piece of wisdom. What is this important piece of wisdom? I'm glad you asked.

It's the fact that whatever you focus on manifests as reality in your life.

You are always focusing on something, whether you are aware of it or not. If I spent some time with you, and heard your history, I could tell you what you are focusing on. How? By looking at the results you are getting in your life. The results you get are always the result of your focus.

The problem is this focus is usually not conscious focus; it's automatic or subconscious focus. We subconsciously focus on something we don't want, and then when we get it we feel like a victim and don't even stop to think that we created it in the first place. And what is more, we don't realize we could choose to create something completely different if we could only get out of the cycle of subconsciously focusing on something other than what we want.

If you have a significant negative emotional experience (say, for instance, a relationship in which you are abused or mistreated in some way), a part of you is going to say: "Okay, I get it. There are people out there who can and will hurt me. Relationships can be dangerous and painful. I have to watch out for these people [or sometimes,

31

relationships in general] and avoid them." Unfortunately, to watch out for them and avoid them, you have to focus your mind on "people who could hurt me," or "bad relationships," and that focus draws more of what you don't want to you...AND...actually makes these things you don't want (at least initially) attractive to you, so when they appear in your life you are drawn to them. This is why many people keep having one relationship after another with the same person, but in different bodies. This, of course, applies to everything, not just relationships. I'm just using relationships as an example.

Focusing on what you do not want, ironically, makes it happen. Focusing on not being poor makes you poor. Focusing on not making mistakes causes you to make mistakes. Focusing on not having a bad relationship creates bad relationships. Focusing on not being depressed makes you depressed. Focusing on not smoking makes you want to smoke. And so on. I think you get the idea. The mind will create what you focus on both GOOD and BAD!!!

The truth is your mind cannot tell the difference between something you think about or focus on that you DO want, and something you think about or focus on but do NOT want. The mind is a goal-seeking mechanism, and an extremely effective one at that. Already, all the time, it is elegantly and precisely creating exactly what you focus on. You are already a World Champion Expert at creating whatever you focus on. You couldn't get any better at it, and you don't need to get any better at it.

When you focus on anything, your mind says: "Okay, we can do that," and starts figuring out how to do it. It doesn't ask whether you're focusing on it because you want it or because you do not want it. It ALWAYS assumes you want what you focus on and then it goes and makes it happen. The more frequent and the more intense the focus, the faster and more completely you will create what you have focused on, which is why intense negative experiences create intense focus on what you do not want, and tend to make you re-create what you don't want, over and over.

Most of the time, for most people, all the focusing and thinking is going by at warp speed, on automatic, without much, if any, conscious intention. Your job is to learn how to direct this power by consciously directing your focus to the outcomes you want. Once you do, everything changes. This does, however, take some work, because at first you have to swim upstream against the current of your old, unconscious habits, and the current can be swift and strong. Trained observation actually teaches you to focus on what you want.

First, you have to discover all the things you focus on that you do not want, and I'm willing to bet there are quite a few -- way more than you think. To the degree you're getting what you don't want, you are focusing, albeit subconsciously, on what you don't want.

Spend some time over the next few weeks making a list of all the things you do NOT want as you notice yourself thinking about them.

Second, you have to get very clear about what you DO want. Then, you have to examine each of the things you want and be sure they are not just something you do NOT want in disguise. For instance, saying "I want a relationship where I am treated well" would not even be an issue if you had not had relationships where you were

33

not treated well, and even in making this seemingly positive statement you are focusing on not wanting to be mistreated. Saying "I want a reliable car" wouldn't even come up if you weren't focusing on the fact that you don't want a car that breaks down and needs a lot of repairs.

After you've sorted out the things you habitually focus on that you do not want, and know what you do want, you have to begin to notice each time you think about an outcome you do not want, and consciously change your thinking, right in that moment, so you are instead focusing on what you do want.

Remember, you do NOT have to avoid things to be happy and get what you want. The urge to avoid something is a result of having had a negative emotional experience regarding that thing, and trying to avoid things requires you to focus on them, which tells your brain to create them. Not good.

You will be surprised how often you are thinking about what you do not want, how difficult it is to catch yourself doing it every time, and -- most of all – how difficult it is to switch your thinking to what you DO want. There is a strong momentum to keep thinking about that thing you want to avoid. As I said, the current is strong and swift, especially at first.

The solution? Practice, practice, practice. Persistence, persistence, persistence!!!

It's a very good idea to write down what you want, very specifically, so that your Fairy Godmother, were she to read it, would know exactly what to give you without any additional explanation.

Then, read what you have written to yourself, preferably out loud, several times a day, while seeing yourself, in your mind, already having what you want.

Believing is seeing and not the other way around as the world teaches you!

The more emotion you can bring to it, the better. Then, take whatever action is available to begin moving toward what you want. A good time to do this reading and visualizing is when you first wake up and before you go to bed.

I know this is work. Do it anyway. There is a price for everything, and this is the price you must pay to get what you want. Be prepared to pay it. It will be worth it, I promise. And be prepared to pay for a while before you get results. Stick with it.

Another way to change your focus is to ask questions. As an example, I'll ask you one right now. What did you have for breakfast this morning? To answer this question (even to just internally process the question), you had to shift your focus from whatever your mind was focused on (hopefully, to what I am teaching) to today's breakfast.

This means that to change your focus, all you have to do is...ask yourself a question!

It also means you better be careful what questions you ask yourself. Good questions include "How can I get X?" "How can I do X?" "How can I be X?" By asking these kinds of questions, you get your mind to focus on what you want to have, do, or be. Then, your mind takes over and answers the question...solves the problem...and creates what you want. You just have to provide the focus, take whatever action presents itself, and be persistent (some things take time).

I would do away with questions like "What's wrong with me?" or "Why can't I find someone to love me?" and so on. Your mind will find an answer to any question you give it, including these disempowering questions.

Learn to say "How can I...?" when you don't know what to do, instead of "I can't," and (if you are persistent in asking) you will receive the answer, every time. Learn to be conscious in what you focus on and your whole life will change.

This all may seem very utopian to you, or overly simplistic, or like a lot of work. I assure you it is not utopian (it's the way all successful people think), it IS simple, but not simplistic, and yes, it is work, at first. The great Napoleon Hill, who spent over 60 years studying the most effective and most successful people of the 20th century, concluded that -- without exception -- "whatever the mind can conceive and believe, it can achieve." He at first suspected there had to be exceptions, but toward the end of his life he said he had to admit he had not found ANY.

Let's go over that again: "Whatever the mind can conceive and believe it can achieve."

It will take some time to learn how to consciously focus your mind. It will require some effort. You will fail many times, and it will seem difficult. But at a certain point you will "get it" and at that point it will become as automatic as the unconscious focusing you have been doing. When that happens, a whole new universe of power will open to you.

More on Focusing

"And be not conformed to this age, but be transformed by the renewing of your mind, in order to prove by you what is the good and pleasing and perfect will of God."

The one thing in your life you can command is your own mind. Whatever negative people and situations you face, you can always choose a positive attitude. But doing so requires a firm, strong commitment.

Helpful: Begin by writing a self-convincing creed – I believe I can direct and control my emotions, intellect and habits with the intention of developing a positive mental attitude. Post it where you'll see it when you get up in the morning. Read it during the day, and say it aloud. Speaking an intention reinforces it. Choose a "self-motivator" – a meaningful phrase tailored to help you reach your positive thinking goals. Examples:

- Counter discouragement with the phrase "Every problem contains the seed of its own solution."

- Fight procrastination with "Do it now."

Keep your self-motivators nearby – in your pocket or on your desk – and repeat them throughout the day to instill these important new values.

Develop A Life Plan. Setting short and long-term goals each day creates a road map for your life. But only set GOOD goals!!! What is a good goal? One where you are 100% in control and one that is founded in love! A goal of raising good, healthy and prosperous children is a bad goal because you are not in control of what your kids choose. See the important difference? The goal is noble but it is not a good goal.

You identify where you're going, focus your mind on getting there and avoid many wrong turns.

Helpful: Use the D-E-S-I-R-E formula as a goal-setting guideline...

- **D**etermine what you want. Be exact, and express the goal positively. Say what you want to be or do rather than what you don't want.

- **E**valuate what you'll give in return. How much work will you do to turn your plan into action?

- **S**et a date for your goal. Be realistic, allowing enough time without postponing it too long.

- **I**dentify a step by step plan. Devise immediate, small steps to get started.

- **R**epeat your plan in writing.

- **E**ach and every day, morning and evening, read your plan aloud as you picture yourself already having achieved your goals.

Writing out your daily goals helps maintain your motivation. Keep them in your pocket or purse to read frequently throughout the day.

The Power of Visualization

Because visual images reach into our deepest mental levels, I have found pictures to be profound motivational tools. Why? Remember the mind holds everything as pictures!

Helpful: Make a list of personal qualities you want to develop...write down the names of people with whom you would like to have better relationships. Now clip pictures from magazines and newspapers that symbolize your goals.

Example: If generosity is your chosen quality, you could use a photo of someone with an outstretched hand.

Put the pictures where you'll see them everyday...and believe that you will get what you have visualized. You may also create your own "mental pictures" to defeat negative thoughts, such as dwelling on past reversals. Maintain A Positive Focus. Giving yourself positive experiences actually reinforces your positive attitude. Examples...

- Treat your five senses every day. Listen to your favorite music, taste a food you love, enjoy a beautiful view, etc.

- Cultivate a sense of humor. Laughter relaxes tension, and seeing the funny side of things helps you take yourself less seriously.

- Smile when you feel like frowning. Smile at yourself in the mirror. If this makes you laugh at yourself, the smile will be that much more real.

Now realize the optimistic face you show the world creates positive thoughts about you in everyone you meet.

How to Train Your Subconscious Mind
Did you know that often the difference between success and failure is the ability to train your mind to focus on achieving your goals and not focus on problems? It's been proven by researchers and by some of the most successful people in the world.

Getting your mind to focus and concentrate on success - so that it finds solutions instead of focusing on the problems is usually the difference between success and failure. But how do you do this?

I'm about to show you how. I'll outline the importance of training your mind, how to start directing your subconscious mind, and how to keep your mind focused so that you constantly achieve your goals and live the life you want. Disciplining your mind so that it is focused on your goals is crucial to your success. If your mind is not trained to focus on and achieve your goals then you really have little chance of success. Your conscious mind is a direct link to your subconscious mind.

So if your mind is focused on your goals and is trained to achieve those goals then your subconscious mind will also be focused on those goals and will attract the situations and opportunities for you to achieve the success you want. It's really that simple.

The minute you get distracted for a prolonged period - you lose sight of your objective and fail to accomplish those goals. In order for to enjoy success - the mind has to be regularly focused on your goals - you can't stay focused for short bursts and expect to get results.

Think of it this way, your riding in a car driven by your personal driver and every time your driver asks you where you want to go you simply say: "I don't know. Wherever you want to go is fine with me." Then when your driver takes you to the place of his choice you complain and say: "I don't want to be here, take me somewhere else." And again you say you don't know where you want to go.

Can you see the confusion you would create? Can you see how you would never get to where you want to go because you haven't trained your driver to automatically take you where you want to go? You haven't given him the proper instructions.

Your mind and subconscious mind work the same way. If you don't train your mind to focus on your goals then your subconscious mind cannot create the situations that will help you achieve those goals. When you keep changing your mind, when you are not clear on what you want - your subconscious gets confused - and you end up exactly where you don't want to be.

Let's go back to the example of your personal driver. Wouldn't it be a lot easier and more comfortable if you told your driver where you wanted to go - or even better - your driver knew where you wanted to go ahead of time? But that will only happen when you train your driver by repeatedly telling him where you want to go on a regular basis.

Your subconscious mind is your driver. Your subconscious gets its instructions from your thoughts and beliefs. Give your subconscious the right instructions and it will take you where ever you want to go in life. When your mind is focused on your goals you direct your subconscious to create opportunities for you to achieve your goals. Your responsibility is to follow up on these opportunities.

How You Can Train Your Mind
Believe it or not I get a lot of calls and emails everyday from people who want to achieve their goals but simply can't get their mind to focus on the tasks that need to be done to have the success that they want. This happens

because the mind is simply not used to focusing on your goals and following up with completing those tasks. So how do you get your mind to change? How do you train your mind?

The first step is to get the mind to stop doing what it is used to doing - or break the pattern that you've been following for so long. This will require some effort - but the reward will allow you to live the life you want and enjoy the level of success that you want.

To re-train your mind and direct your subconscious mind you start by paying more attention - so that when you see yourself getting distracted and not following up on things that you wanted to do - you take a step to break the pattern. You can break the pattern by doing something else. For example: you can start following up on what you had planned to do, you can create a list and follow up with it regularly to see if you are on track.

One thing that always works is to think about your goals every morning. As you're in bed, think about your goals and think about what you can do to achieve them during the day. If you find that you constantly say: "I don't know what do to to achieve my goals." Then you're not looking for answers in the right place.

Take a look at what other people have done to achieve similar goals and see if you can follow the same process. For example: If you want to make more money take a look at someone else who has made a lot of money and see what they've done. Can you follow their process? Maybe you can even talk to them about the process? If you want to meet someone and be in a healthy relationship, talk to a friend who is in a successful relationship and find out what they did. By doing the above exercises you train your mind to focus on finding solutions while at the same time you direct your subconscious mind to create the opportunities for you to succeed. And - you begin to create a new pattern of thinking and you start to train the mind to work differently. You're now telling your driver where you want to go. This eliminates the confusion and allows you to achieve your goals.

You're not going to magically get your mind to focus or concentrate without you taking some form of action. When you finally do take some action your mind will still resist - but as you continue taking action the resistance will subside - REPITITION. So what action can you take? First start with the exercise I just outlined above. Next - meditate. Meditation is one of the best ways to relax and calm your mind while training it to focus on what you want. When you meditate you actually start to clear the clutter that dominates your mind.

Make the Time
Finally it seems a lot of people have come to believe that they just don't have the time to achieve their goals. If you are one of the many who have such a belief then you've really convinced yourself that your goals are not worthy of your time; because if they were you would make the time for them. I'm not talking about spending an entire day or even a few hours. It's only a few minutes at different intervals. Why try to get everything crammed into one hour? Why not try to think about your goals at different intervals during the day? For example: you may have a few minutes while you're taking a walk - think of your achieving your goals. You could also do this while you're taking a shower, driving, walking, anytime. Here's a suggestion; the next time you are driving or taking a

shower, pay attention to your thoughts. Are these thoughts actually working for your or against you? Would it be better to focus on your goals or keep recycling the negative clutter or junk in your head? The choice is yours - and taking action is really about taking a small step. You don't need to spend hours meditating. Even if you simply mediated for 5 or 10 minutes a day you'd be able to increase your ability to concentrate and focus by a 100-percent within a matter of days! Do it for weeks or months and you'll have dramatic results!

How to Put Your Mind to Sleep Quickly and Rest Completely

If you often lay awake, unable to put your mind to rest while you're tossing and turning, you're going to love what you're about to read, because I'm about to share with you one of the most powerful methods for quickly shutting off your mind, and drifting off to sleep.

As you may already know, your mind must be in the Alpha brain-wave stage to fall asleep. This is the stage your mind enters you're still conscious, but your body and begin to relax. It enables your more rampant and conscious mind to turn off as you enter the realm of sleep. We all know how it feels... when you're lying awake in bed trying to fall asleep, it seems like your mind is running on hyper-speed. It's almost like you're thinking 10 times faster than when you're just normally awake and alert. In fact, if you experience this often, I can tell you for a fact that your mind IS working harder than it is when you're not trying to fall asleep, and there is a very good reason for it, here's why this happens. In my books and articles on sleep, I often teach a principle: "What you focus on expands." You see, your mind responds to focus, and it goes hand in hand with the law of momentum. What is the law of momentum? Quite simply:

"Energy in motion, tends to STAY in motion"

"Energy stopped, tends to STAY stopped"

In other words, if you take action in your life, and begin to create success, you will experience more and more success every day. Success breeds success. On the other hand, if you sit your butt down on the couch to watch TV and say, "Aww, just one show, I'll only watch one show," very soon you'll be sitting there for four hours, and you'll watch five or six shows.

The law of momentum is everywhere in life, in physics, with your body, and most importantly, with your "thoughts." You see, your thinking is very predictable; it all works on the law of focus and momentum. Your mind is like a big ball of potential thinking energy, just waiting for you to give it a direction to think wildly into. It awaits and responds your every command. It's an exceptional tool except, most of us aren't very experienced at "controlling" this amazing tool. In fact, a lot people aren't even aware that they can control it! And this is where sleep problems come in.

Imagine your mind like a giant overflowing lake that's just waiting for an outlet to pour into... Slowly, when it finds an outlet, it begins with a trickle of water. That trickle turns into a stream. Then, that stream turns into a small river. Pretty soon, the small river is a giant unstoppable waterfall. Your thoughts work in the same way when you're "trying" to fall asleep.

For example, you're lying in bed, frustrated, forcing your mind to not think. "I just want to get some sleep! Stop thinking! Okay, starting now... I won't think anymore. No think... nothing. My life is nothing... If only I would finally get motivated in my job maybe I would finally create the income to start traveling instead of dealing with these problems. Problems, how can I... Ahh, I'm thinking again! Stop it!"

You get even more frustrated, and repeat the process over again in a few minutes. So how do you stop it? It's easy, you see, you can easily control your thinking, except most people aren't aware of the tools necessary! The good news is, I'm about to give you the 3-step handbook to controlling your mind. Here are the 3-universal steps that will enable you to not only stop thinking; you'll also be able to lower your brain-waves into the alpha brain-state, which will quickly let you enter sleep...

Awareness
The first step to changing anything is becoming aware that it's happening, especially if it's your mind. Pretend your mind is racing, and you finally realize that you're thinking... Most people at this stage get extremely frustrated and "try" to force the mind into submission. It doesn't work! Why? Because, what you focus on expands. The more frustrated you get, the more you're focusing on frustration, so you'll get even MORE frustration and more thinking... on and on!

So the first step is to simply become "aware" of the fact that you're thinking. Nothing more. When you notice that you're thinking, smile to yourself, and say, "I just noticed myself thinking... Interesting..." Now notice what happens inside of you when you do this... something VERY profound. If "I" just noticed "myself" thinking, perhaps there are really two completely separate

46

identities running your life? There is the "I" and there is the "self."

The "I", is the real you, the higher being, the "I" behind the mind, that runs the show, the heart, the soul, the true conscious being, the choice maker.

The "self" is the mind; if left to run the show, it will run in endless circles until the edge of insanity.

The moment you do this, the moment you become "aware" - you are no longer a slave to your mind. You have won. After you become aware... do nothing, just lay there for 3 seconds and notice how it feels to be present in who you really are, not the mind, but you, the "I" - there is a great feeling of peace behind that presence in the "I." Why? Because when you are aware like this, you're aware of the power of your choice making. You now have the power of choice.

Relaxed Focus
"What you focus on expands." Now that you have become aware of your thinking, all you have to do is "direct" your mind into a place that will bring you into a deep, deep place of relaxation. Think about it, if before your mind will relentlessly race into any direction you give it; why not pick a direction that will give you peace and restful sleep?

But, most people don't know what that direction really is. It's really easy. If you focus on anything your body does or feels subconsciously, you will begin to become more and more realized. For example your breathing, the feeling of the pillow on your head, the sounds of nature outside (unless you live in the city), the warmth of your body. These are all things that happen, yet your conscious mind doesn't think about them.

As you know, "What you focus on expands"... So what would happen if you focused on something that is happening in your "subconscious"? That's right, your conscious thinking would diminish, and your subconscious mind would begin to take over the entire process of you falling asleep! It really is that simple, and it works every-time.

The easiest one is your breathing. And I promise you if you just try this tonight, you will be shocked when you wake up in the morning: "Wow! It worked!"

Repetition

As I said, the easiest one to focus on is your breathing. In the beginning, you'll find this easier said than done. Let me walk you through it.

- Begin by taking your focus onto your breathing. Take a deep breath in. Hold it for a short while, and slowly exhale...

- Count "1"

- Breathe in again... hold it shortly, exhale slowly, and count...

- "2"

Why count? Because I guarantee you, in the very beginning, you may find it challenging to hold your focus. In fact, you'll be surprised as you may not even make it to "5" the first time. This is because your conscious ever-thinking mind will butt in and interrupt. You may randomly go off into a barrage of thoughts again. If this happens, and it very well may, what do you do?

Simply become aware, and begin focusing on your breathing again. Guess what happens? As you become aware, 2 or 3 times... your mind will give up. I guarantee you, beyond the shadow of a doubt, when you get to "10" or "15" breaths you will feel a wave of relaxation in your body. This is the silent "click" as your mind shifts from the high frequency Beta brain-waves into Alpha brain-waves. Your subconscious mind will do the rest!

Chapter 2 – Inductive Reasoning

The Inductive Methodology

Inductive reasoning (as opposed to *deductive* reasoning) is a form of reasoning where the premises seek to supply strong evidence for (but not absolute proof of) the truth of the conclusion. It is important to note that the evidence can be completely wrong and conclusion flawed because the evidence is wrong.

While a deductive argument supposes certainty, an inductive argument supposes *probability*, based upon the evidence given. It is interesting to note that inductive reasoning is the basis of most scientific theories eg; Darwinism, Big bang theory and Einstein's Relativity theory. Systematic science first proposes a theory and when this theory cannot be disproven (in science this is called falsification) then it becomes a law of science.

The definition of inductive reasoning is much more complicated than a simple progression from particular or individual instances to broader generalizations. The premises of an inductive logical argument dictate to some degree support (inductive probability) for the conclusion but do not entail it; or in other words, they suggest truth but do not ensure it. There remains the possibility of moving from general statements to individual instances.

50

Many dictionaries have varied definitions of inductive reasoning with the majority defining it as reasoning that derives general principles from specific observations, though some sources disagree with this usage.

Inductive reasoning is most always uncertain for it only deals in degrees where given the premises; the conclusion is *credible* according to some theory of evidence. Examples include Dempster–Shafer theory, or Einstein's probability theory with rules for inference such as Bayes' rule. Inductive reasoning does not rely on universals holding over a closed domain of discourse to draw conclusions, so it can be applicable even in cases of epistemic uncertainty (technical issues with this may arise however; for example, the second axiom of probability is a closed-world assumption).

A statistical syllogism is an example of inductive reasoning:

- Almost all people of Africa are taller than 26 inches
- Tsimbo is a person
- Therefore, Tsimbo is almost certainly African and taller than 26 inches

As a stronger example:

- All biological life forms that we know of depend on liquid water to exist.
- Therefore, if we discover a new biological life form it will probably depend on liquid water to exist.

This argument could have been made every time a new biological life form was found, and would have been correct every time; however, it is still possible that in the future a biological life form not requiring water could be discovered.

As a result, the argument may be stated less formally as:

- All biological life forms that we know of depend on liquid water to exist.
- All biological life probably depends on liquid water to exist.

Understanding Inductive Reasoning

There are varying degrees of strength and weakness in inductive reasoning, and various types including statistical syllogism, arguments from example, causal inferences, simple inductions, and inductive generalizations. They can have part to whole relations, extrapolations, or predictions.

Some examples of inductive reasoning include:

- Jane and Rob are friends. Jane likes to dance, cook and write. Rob likes to dance and cook. Therefore it can be assumed he also likes to write.
- Jillian leaves for school at 7:00 a.m. and is on time. Jillian assumes, then, that she will always be on time if she leaves at 7:00 a.m.
- Sam is a teacher. All teachers are nice. Therefore, it can be assumed that Sam is nice.

- All cats that you have observed purr. Therefore, every cat must purr.
- All students that have been taught by Mrs. Schneider are right handed. So, Mrs. Schneider assumes that all students are right handed.
- All basketball players are tall, so all basketball players must be tall.
- All women in one area wear high heels, so all women must wear high heels.
- Sheila is a doctor. Doctors are smart. Sheila is assumed to be smart.
- Jeff is a financial analyst. Individuals with professions in finance are very serious people. Jeff is a very serious person.
- Jack is a bartender. Bartenders are friendly. Jack is assumed to be friendly.
- All brown dogs are small dogs. Therefore, all small dogs are brown.
- All kids like to play with Legos. All kids, therefore, enjoy playing with Legos.
- The water at the beach has always been about 68 degrees in July. It is July. The water will be about 68 degrees.
- All law enforcement officers are under 50 years old. Jules is a law enforcement officer. Jules is under 50 years old.
- Margo and Sally are friends. Margo enjoys fishing, running and rock climbing. Sally likes fishing and rock climbing. Sally must also like running.
- Barney is a baseball player. All baseball players can make it to first base in at least 4 seconds.

Barney can make it to first base in at least 4 seconds.

- Jay is a football player. All football players weigh more than 170 pounds. Jay weighs more than 170 pounds.
- All observed lacrosse players are tall and thin. Geoff plays lacrosse. It is assumed that Geoff is tall and thin.
- All little dogs are "yappy." Bart has a small dog. His dog barks frequently at a high pitched level.
- All cats in the area are brown. Tinsel is a cat. Tinsel is brown.
- All houses on the Main Street are falling apart. Cheryl lives on Main Street. Her house is falling apart.
- Jesse is a dancer. Dancers are thin and tall. Jesse is thin and tall.
- Mark is a sumo wrestler. Sumo wrestlers weigh a lot. Mark weighs a lot.

Now you can see how inductive reasoning works and the types of things you can discern using inductive reasoning.

Now let's move on to deductive reasoning…

1. Which of the following best describes deductive reasoning?

A. using logic to draw conclusions based on accepted statements

B. accepting the meaning of a term without Definition

C. defining mathematical terms to correspond with physical objects

D. inferring a general truth by examining a number of specific examples

By now you should begin to see that deductive reasoning is the better form of reason since it is based on validity and facts while inductive reasoning is based on assumption of facts.

Deductive reasoning is the basic form of valid reasoning. Deductive reasoning or deduction, starts out with a general statement, or hypothesis, and examines the possibilities to reach a specific, logical conclusion or theory. The scientific method uses deduction to test hypotheses and theories. Once a theory is falsified or disproven it becomes a law of science.

Using deductive reasoning, if something is true of a class of things in general, it is also true for all members of that class. For example, "All women are mortal. Betty is a woman. Therefore, Betty is mortal." For deductive reasoning to be a sound form of reasoning, the hypothesis must be correct. It is assumed that the premises, "All women are mortal" and "Betty is a woman" are true. Therefore, the conclusion is logical and true.

Using deductive reasoning, it's possible to come to a logical conclusion even if the generalization is not true. If the generalization is wrong, it is possible that the conclusion may be logical, but it may also be untrue. For example, the argument, "All bald eagles are not really bald. Sajack is a bald eagle Therefore, Sajack is not really bald," is valid logically but it is untrue because the original statement is false.

The term "inductive reasoning" refers to reasoning that takes specific information and makes a broader generalization that is considered probable, allowing for the fact that the conclusion may not be accurate.

Chapter 4 – Intellectual versus Emotional Decisions

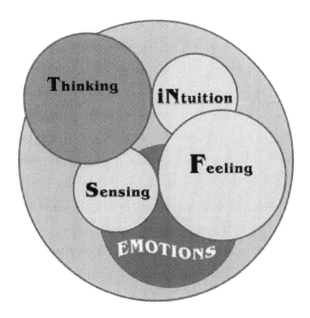

One of the first things my dad taught me as I was growing up was, "Never make an emotional decision intellectually nor make an intellectual decision emotionally!"

And this is very good advice.

Emotions are rarely based on fact but they are based on feelings. Why should you keep them separate? Emotional decisions can lead to addiction.

Here are some excellent articles for you to read that will make the distinctions clearly and allow you to slowly digest the content of each article at your own pace. One you understand the difference between emotions and intellect, a good many things will become better focused in your daily lives:

http://www.cell.com/trends/cognitive-sciences//retrieve/pii/S1364661304003171?cc=y

Abstract

Questions about the nature of normative and atypical development in adolescence have taken on special significance in the last few years, as scientists have begun to recast old portraits of adolescent behavior in the light of new knowledge about brain development. Adolescence is often a period of especially heightened vulnerability as a consequence of potential disjunctions between developing brain, behavioral and cognitive systems that mature along different timetables and under the control of both common and independent biological processes. Taken together, these developments reinforce the emerging understanding of adolescence as a critical or sensitive period for a reorganization of regulatory systems, a reorganization that is fraught with both risks and opportunities.

http://cercor.oxfordjournals.org/content/10/3/295.short

Abstract

The somatic marker hypothesis provides a systems-level neuroanatomical and cognitive framework for decision making and the influence on it by emotion. The key idea of this hypothesis is that decision making is a process that is influenced by marker signals that arise in bioregulatory processes, including those that express themselves in emotions and feelings. This influence can occur at multiple levels of operation, some of which occur consciously and some of which occur non-consciously. Here we review studies that confirm various predictions from the hypothesis. The orbitofrontal cortex represents one critical structure in a neural system subserving decision making. Decision making is not mediated by the orbitofrontal cortex alone, but arises from large-scale systems that include other cortical and subcortical components. Such structures include the amygdala, the somatosensory/insular cortices and the peripheral nervous system. Here we focus only on the role of the orbitofrontal cortex in decision making and emotional processing, and the relationship between emotion, decision making and other cognitive functions of the frontal lobe, namely working memory.

Abstract

Collective knowledge building is a key strategic task for firms' success today. But creating and sharing knowledge are intangible activities that can neither be supervised nor forced out of people. They happen only when individuals cooperate voluntarily. A key challenge facing strategic management is obtaining the voluntary cooperation of individuals as firms formulate and implement their strategic decisions. This essay draws on the rich body of procedural justice research to address this critical issue. We argue that when people feel their strategic decision-making processes are fair, they display a high level of voluntary cooperation based on their attitudes of trust and commitment. Conversely, when people feel that the processes are unfair, they refuse to cooperate by hoarding ideas and dragging their feet in conceiving and executing strategic decisions. We further develop this argument into team performance wherein the attitudinal and behavioral effects of procedural justice are corroborated with theory and initial evidence of their bottom-line performance consequences. We then build a theory, which we call intellectual and emotional recognition theory that can explain why procedural justice invokes the side of human behavior that goes beyond outcome-driven self-interests and that is so critical in the knowledge economy.

http://www.sciencedirect.com/science/article/pii/S027826
2603002859

Abstract

Most theories of choice assume that decisions derive from an assessment of the future outcomes of various options and alternatives through some type of cost-benefit analyses. The influence of emotions on decision-making is largely ignored. The studies of decision-making in neurological patients who can no longer process emotional information normally suggest that people make judgments not only by evaluating the consequences and their probability of occurring, but also and even sometimes primarily at a gut or emotional level. Lesions of the ventromedial (which includes the orbitofrontal) sector of the prefrontal cortex interfere with the normal processing of "somatic" or emotional signals, while sparing most basic cognitive functions. Such damage leads to impairments in the decision-making process, which seriously compromise the quality of decisions in daily life. The aim of this paper is to review evidence in support of "The Somatic Marker Hypothesis," which provides a systems-level neuroanatomical and cognitive framework for decision-making and suggests that the process of decision-making depends in many important ways on neural substrates that regulate homeostasis, emotion, and feeling. The implications of this theoretical framework for the normal and abnormal development of the orbitofrontal cortex are also discussed.

http://link.springer.com/article/10.1023/A:1021223113233

Abstract

Although metabolic abnormalities in the orbitofrontal cortex have been observed in substance dependent individuals (SDI) for several years, very little attention was paid to the role of this brain region in addiction. However, patients with damage to the ventromedial (VM) sector of the prefrontal cortex and SDI show similar behaviors. (1) They often deny, or they are not aware, that they have a problem. (2) When faced with a choice to pursue a course of action that brings an immediate reward at the risk of incurring future negative consequences, they choose the immediate reward and ignore the future consequences. Studies of patients with bilateral lesions of the VM prefrontal cortex support the view that the process of decision-making depends in many important ways on neural substrates that regulate homeostasis, emotion, and feeling. Parallel lines of study have revealed that VM cortex dysfunction is also evident in subgroups of individuals who are addicted to substances. Thus, understanding the neural mechanisms of decision-making has direct implications for understanding disorders of addiction and pathological gambling, and the switch from a controlled to uncontrolled and compulsive behavior. On the clinical front, the approach to treat addictive disorders has been dominated by a diagnostic system that focuses on behaviors, physical symptoms, or choice of drugs. The article emphasizes the concept of using neurocognitive criteria for subtyping addictive disorders. This is a significant paradigm shift with significant implications for guiding diagnosis and treatment. Using neurocognitive criteria could lead to more accurate subtyping of addictive disorders, and perhaps serve as a guide for more specific, and potentially more successful, behavioral and pharmacological interventions.

*****

The following article makes some very valid points and is worth a good read.

Decisions Are Emotional, not Logical: The Neuroscience behind Decision Making
By Jim Camp

http://bigthink.com/experts-corner/decisions-are-emotional-not-logical-the-neuroscience-behind-decision-making

Think of a situation where you had bulletproof facts, reason, and logic on your side, and believed there was absolutely no way the other person could say no to your perfectly constructed argument and proposal. To do so would be impossible, you figured, because there was no other logical solution or answer.

And then the other person dug in his heels and refused to budge. He wasn't swayed by your logic. Were you flabbergasted?

This is similar to what many negotiators do when they sit down at the table to hammer out a deal. They come armed with facts, and they attempt to use logic to sway the other party. They figure that by piling on the data and using reason to explain their side of the situation, they can construct a solution that is simply irrefutable—and get the other party to say yes.

They're doomed to fail, however, because decision-making isn't logical, it's emotional, according to the latest findings in neuroscience.

A few years ago, neuroscientist Antonio Damasio made a groundbreaking discovery. He studied people with damage in the part of the brain where emotions are generated. He found that they seemed normal, except that they were not able to feel emotions. But they all had something peculiar in common: they couldn't make decisions. They could describe what they should be doing in logical terms, yet they found it very difficult to make even simple decisions, such as what to eat. Many decisions have pros and cons on both sides—shall I have the chicken or the turkey? With no rational way to decide, these test subjects were unable to arrive at a decision.

So at the point of decision, emotions are very important for choosing. In fact even with what we believe are logical decisions, the very point of choice is arguably always based on emotion.

This finding has enormous implications for negotiation professionals. People who believe they can build a case for their side using reason are doomed to be poor negotiators, because they don't understand the real factors that are driving the other party to come to a decision. Those who base their negotiation strategy on logic end up relying on assumptions, guesses, and opinions. If my side of the argument is logical, they figure, then the other side can't argue with it and is bound to come around to my way of thinking. The problem is you can't assume that the other party will see things your way.

What the negotiator can and must do, however, is create a vision for the other side to bring about discovery and decision on their part. In the end, your opponent will make the decision because he wants to. Getting him to want to, using the step-by-step methodology that is part of the Camp System, is the job of the negotiator—not trying to convince him with reason.

You don't tell your opponent what to think or what's best. You help them discover for themselves what feels right and best and most advantageous to them. Their ultimate decision is based on self-interest. That's emotional. I want this. This is good for me and my side.

There's a detailed and systematic way to go about building vision the right way. But in general, if you can get the other party to reveal their problems, pain, and unmet objectives, then you can build a vision for them of their problem, with you and your proposal as the solution. They won't make their decision because it is logical. They'll make their decision because you have helped them feel that it's to their advantage to do so.

* * * * *

Jim Camp is founder and CEO of The Camp Negotiation Institute, with more than 400 students from 24 countries enrolled in its Team Member courses. He is author of two bestselling books published by Crown, Start with No and NO: The Only System of Negotiation You Need for Work or Home, which have been translated into 12 languages, and a new 6-CD audio program "The Power of No," produced by Nightingale-Conant. He was recently a featured panelist at Harvard's 2012 Negotiation & Leadership Conference.

*****

Read the above article multiple times to thoroughly understand how emotions affect decisions.

Chapter 5 – Why We Must Decide

Another adage my dad taught me when I was growing up was, "In every man's life one must decide; the brave man makes a choice while the coward steps aside."

Why we must decide is an important topic. Learning simply cannot take place unless the mind decides what is truth and what is not truth. The mind is not interested in validating truth; perception of truth is stronger than the actual truth itself. Perception rules! And remember from Chapter 1, the mind is very gullible to a point where it cannot tell the difference between reality and fantasy.

Many decisions we make daily are not conscious decisions but subconscious ones based on belief systems already residing in your subconscious. If your underlying belief systems are wrong then your decisions will be wrong.

Here is an example:

Recently an article appeared where a pastor of a Christian church got a tattoo. The uproar from the congregation was so vehement that collectively the pastor was asked to resign.

Now many of you will think, "What's the big thing about a tattoo? Everybody nowadays has one or more."

The uproar came from the congregation based on biblical teachings not to get a tattoo.

<u>Leviticus 19:28</u> You shall not make any cuts on your body for the dead or tattoo yourselves: I am the LORD.

Yes, it is an accepted practice to get tattoos but according to the church's teaching this is a sin. Once you understand the context of the uproar you are free to decide that tattooing is a sin or it is not a sin. You now have both sides of the argument.

The example above requires you to decide what side of the argument is right but your decision should be based on fact and not feelings. Can you do this? It is easy to say to yourself, "The pastor has every right to get a tattoo," and ignore the fact that in his profession he does not have the right to go against the laws of God.

Your decision does not affect the argument; your decision does affect how you will behave because your decision becomes a belief system in your subconscious mind and as you learned in Chapter one, belief systems acted upon by thought equals action/behavior/conduct.

You may decide tattoos are okay and hence may even get one because you believe that a tattoo is okay.

You may also decide that it is a sin and hence you will never get a tattoo.

You should quickly see that the human mind strives to decide; to take a stand either pro or con based on information presented to it. This is not a voluntary response to any input into the human mind. The mind is always striving to learn and the belief systems you embrace are accumulated based on the way you decide and your action/behavior/conduct will be affected by what you believe.

Remember the term "acceptance". You must accept voluntarily or involuntarily whatever side of the argument to embrace. Refer back to Chapter 1 and reread the part on acceptance.

Here is a great article for you to consider:

http://www.bain.com/publications/articles/why-we-behave-and-decide-the-way-we-do.aspx

Why we behave—and decide—the way we do

Organizational ailments, such as too much complexity, often interfere with good business decision making and execution. But they aren't the only source of trouble. Even in the best of circumstances, people must ultimately make and execute decisions, and we human beings are even more complicated than a tangled org chart or a messy decision process. We are prisoners of emotions, habits and biases. We choose A rather than B for reasons that we often don't understand. These pitfalls can ensnare individuals who are making decisions; they can also cause groups to go astray.

The good news is that psychologists and behavioral economists have been studying why people decide the way they do. In this article we'll look at individual behaviors, highlighting just four of the many obstacles that these scholars have identified. If you're aware of the traps, you are far less likely to be snared by them—and your decisions and actions will be that much better.

1. Fairness. It's a familiar story, known to behavioral economists as a version of the "ultimatum game." A bored rich lady sits between two strangers—call them Robert and Juliette—on a plane. For entertainment, she offers to give Robert $10,000, with the proviso that he must make a one-time binding offer to give some of it to Juliette. If Juliette accepts Robert's proposed split, they divide the money accordingly. If she rejects it, the rich lady keeps her money, and Robert and Juliette get nothing.

So how much does Robert offer? In theory, he could offer Juliette only $10. A rational person would accept it because it was, after all, free money. In practice—and the experiment has been conducted repeatedly—people in the Juliette role regularly reject any offer that they deem unfair. A powerful moral principle, fairness, plays a big role in decision making, often stronger even than self-interest.

You can see this phenomenon in business as well: any decision that people regard as unfair, such as paying bonuses to executives while laying off lower-level employees, is likely to trigger a sharp reaction.

2. Confirmation bias. This is a version of what psychologists sometimes call "motivated reasoning"—we seek out and believe information that confirms our opinions, while ignoring or downplaying information that contradicts them.

Many experiments have confirmed this tendency. A few years ago, for instance, Drew Westen and colleagues at

Emory University in Atlanta recruited 15 Republicans and 15 Democrats and presented them with contradictory behaviors from the two major candidates in the 2004 US presidential election, along with statements designed to explain the contradictions. For example, George W. Bush once said he "loved" Enron CEO Ken Lay, but after Enron's collapse he was critical of the company and avoided any mention of Lay. The explanation was that he felt betrayed by Lay and was shocked to learn of Enron's corruption. Each set of partisans tended to believe the explanatory statements for their own candidate, while regarding the statements by the opposition candidate as inconsistent.

In big decisions, individuals can easily fall into confirmation bias, jeopardizing the possibility of reaching the best outcome.

3. Framing and anchoring. Every decision depends on information. The structure and reference points of that information shape how the decision maker receives and uses it. Chief executives contemplating an acquisition, for instance, often frame the question as "Why should we do this deal?" and then answer it by focusing on potential but often illusory synergies. If they frame it instead as "How much should we be willing to pay?" the decision can turn out quite differently.

Anchoring—using a predetermined reference point as the launch pad for a decision—is equally powerful. A few years ago, for instance, Wharton School professor Paul J. H. Schoemaker was studying bad loans at a bank in the southern US. He found that bank officers assessing a loan naturally began by determining its current rating and asking themselves whether they should upgrade or downgrade it. Because of the anchoring effect of the current rating, as a report on Schoemaker's work noted, downgrades tended to be incremental adjustments. So "by the time a loan was classified as troubled, it could be too late to take remedial action."

4. Overconfidence. People everywhere tend to see their own abilities in an unrealistically positive light. Some 93% of US drivers famously say they are better than average. Countless sales managers regularly predict double-digit annual gains, especially in the out years, hence the prevalence of hockey-stick forecasts.

Overconfidence often leads to terrible decisions, and not just in business. Consider the invasion of Gallipoli in 1915, which British officers thought would be an easy victory. "Let me bring my lads face to face with Turks in the open field," wrote Commander Sir Ian Hamilton in his diary. "We must beat them every time because British volunteer soldiers are superior individuals to Anatolians, Syrians or Arabs...." The British were decisively defeated at Gallipoli, notes Malcolm Gladwell in the New Yorker, partly because of such overconfidence.

Analyze any bad decision and you are likely to find more than one of these biases at work, each reinforcing the others. Consider the tragic 1986 decision to launch the space shuttle Challenger in spite of unusually cold weather. Confirmation bias? NASA determined that previous flights had been successful, even though the seals on the solid rocket booster showed unexplained signs of erosion. Overconfidence? Management estimated that the chances of shuttle failure were as little as 1 in 100,000—low enough, as the late physicist Richard Feynman pointed out, to "imply that one could put up a shuttle every day for 300 years expecting to lose only one." As for framing, Jim Collins, in How the Mighty Fall, notes that the crucial go/no-go decision in the Challenger situation was framed as, "Can you prove it's unsafe to launch?" Reversing the framing—"Can you prove it's safe to launch?"—might have led to a different decision.

What to do about decision bias? It helps, of course, to be on the lookout for its sources, and to try to compensate accordingly. Organizations can also create robust decision processes that acknowledge and address the biases. They can frame questions in such a way as to pressure-test assumptions. They can explicitly assign the role of devil's advocate, or even create a "red team, blue team" debate so that both sides of a major issue are fully represented. Of course, the human brain is more complex than any organization, and people will doubtless continue to cling to their biases. But robust countermeasures can at least minimize the likelihood that biases will lead to poor decisions.

Paul Rogers is a partner with Bain & Company in London and leads Bain's Global Organization practice. Robert Carse and Todd Senturia are Bain partners based in London and Los Angeles, respectively.

*****

You should now begin to understand that using emotions in your decision making process can skew the facts to a subjective rather than objective condition. I am quite certain that if you look back in your life to where you made poor decisions, you will find that your decisions were based on emotions rather than facts.

Now let's pull it all together and offer you a checklist as to how to make good decisions...

Chapter 6 – Summing It All Up

We have talked about a good many things. The object and goal of this book was to demonstrate different ways people make decisions and offer a better way so now I want to give you a step-by-step blueprint on how to figure things out. Read each step carefully and you may need to reread the entire check list multiple times for it to truly sink in. NOTE: Emotions have their place in our lives and emotions in and of themselves are not wrong. But like everything in life, emotions have their proper place and their place in your decision making process is wrong.

1. Listen to both side of an argument.

Listening is not the same as hearing. If you were standing in the middle of a carnival, your ears hear everything going on around you but your mind "filters" most of it out. Filters reside in the subconscious mind and one of my colleagues wrote a fantastic book I highly recommend:

The Power of Trained Observation
http://www.amazon.com/dp/B00BSRYMGW

One very interesting aspect of this book is how it trains you to place the filters in your "conscious mind" instead of the subconscious mind and hence, you see and hear everything then evaluate it based on facts.

2. Determine what argument is valid using deductive reasoning.

The human mind seeks to decide and in its decision it uses what is called "acceptance" and this was described in Chapter 1. Once any premise or argument is accepted it then becomes a belief system to be acted upon by thought which in turn evokes action/behavior/conduct.

3. If none of the arguments prove valid to you then seek additional information.

77

Even though it may seem that both sides of an argument is presented, it may not appear so to you. In my example In Chapter 5 about the pastor that got a tattoo, the argument that the bible teaches against tattooing the body would not be a valid argument to an atheist. The further argument that tattooing was an accepted social more may also not be valid to an atheist since the argument states nothing about the non-existence of God that is paramount to an atheist's thinking. This would cause the atheist to seek validation in an argument that since an atheist's belief is that God does not exist, it follows that tattooing cannot be forbidden by God. This is a fallacious argument because to state something does not exist is first accepting the fact that it does exist and needs to be falsified or disproved.

4.   If none of the arguments prove valid to you then provide your own argument and proof.

It is quite possible for a person to reject both sides of the argument and provide his/her own argument. Be careful! This can also be a form of denial where you attempt to convince yourself of an argument that suits your own situation. It is rarely based on subjective facts but more often than not based on subjective facts.

5.   In your decision making process use your intellect rather than your emotions.

One of the best examples of this is love versus lust. Most people base their decisions of marrying for example on emotions rather than intellect and this could be a reason for the divorce rate being so high. Ask yourself what your criteria to marry are and list them out on a yellow pad of paper. I will almost guarantee you will be amazed at how many items listed are emotional rather than intellectual.

6. How do you know what you accept as valid is truthful?

This one ought to cause you to think. The is a term in behavioral science called "scarcity thought" where a person believes that someone else is getting what is owed to them and acts accordingly. Scarcity thought is pure emotions and nothing based on fact so if you are accepting an argument as valid but are doing so based on scarcity thought than you are accepting something wrong as factual. Before I accept an argument I check it out to see if it is factual or not. Using the example of the Pastor getting a tattoo again in Chapter 5, it is easy to check the bible and see exactly what verse Leviticus 19:28 says and conversely, it is just as easy to see what the accepted belief is or social more regarding tattooing but just because everybody does it doesn't make it right. Accepting tattooing because everybody does it is called "herd mentality" where you follow what everybody else does because you desire to be accepted.

7. Seek outside sources for to prove validation.

When I buy or sell a car, I just don't look at Kelly Blue Book (kbb.com) to get an idea of what the car is worth. I also go to Autotrader.com and Edmunds.com plus more (just Google "Car valuation guide". My point is to first seek all of the facts to prove any premise as valid and then decide.

8. Be careful where you get your facts.

With the advent of the Internet, people believe that if it is on the Internet then it is real and factual; when the opposite is true. Most things you read on the Internet are pure BS. Do your own thinking and do not allow anything or anybody to influence your decisions. This applies to both secular as well as non-secular thought. In secular thought, anything can be couched to be factual. My dad taught me, "The best lie is always sandwiched between two truths." A good example is politics where the liberals attempt to turn America into a nanny state where all Americans are dependent on the government. They attack the inherent greed in an individual where welfare is easily received and now more people are sitting out of the workplace than are working. The conservatives are fighting this all the way and believe in an individual's right to self-determination.

9. See if you can prove to yourself the opposite premise of the argument even if it is against your current beliefs.

One of my personal tests that I use all of the time is seeing if I can prove the opposite side of the argument even if I believe the other side of the argument is factual and valid. This is a great mind exercise and it gets easier as your mind learns this technique.

*****

It is time to say goodbye and I hope I have assisted you in making better choices and in turn enjoying the benefits of making good choice. If you have any questions just write to me; I will respond – treatpreston@epubwealth.com. Now I have a special gift for you...

I Have a Special Gift for My Readers

I appreciate my readers for without them I am just another author attempting to make a difference. If my book has made a favorable impression please leave me an honest review. Thank you in advance for you participation.

My readers and I have in common a passion for the written word as well as the desire to learn and grow from books.

My special offer to you is a massive ebook library that I have compiled over the years. It contains hundreds of fiction and non-fiction ebooks in Adobe Acrobat PDF format as well as the Greek classics and old literary classics too.

In fact, this library is so massive to completely download the entire library will require over 5 GBs open on your desktop.

Use the link below and scan all of the ebooks in the library. You can select the ebooks you want individually or download the entire library.

The link below does not expire after a given time period so you are free to return for more books rather than clog your desktop. And feel free to give the link to your friends who enjoy reading too.

I thank you for reading my book and hope if you are pleased that you will leave me an honest review so that I can improve my work and or write books that appeal to your interests.

Okay, here is the link…

http://www.epubwealth.com/bookstore-bookstore-services/epubwealth-promotion-download-page/

PS: If you wish to reach me personally for any reason you may simply write to mailto:support@epubwealth.com.

I answer all of my emails so rest assured I will respond.

Meet the Author

Dr. Treat Preston is a behavioral scientist specializing in all types of relationships and associated problems, psychological triggers as applied to commercial advertising and marketing, and energy psychology. He is a best-selling author with numerous books dealing on publishing, behavioral science, marketing and more. He is also one of the lead research scientists with AppliedMindSciences.com, the mind research unit of ForensicsNation.com. As a Senior Forensics Investigator, Dr. Preston profile perpetrators of all types of crimes and assists the ForensicsNation team of investigators identify and track down cyber criminals of all types all the way to apprehension and incarceration.

He and his wife Cynthia reside in Auburn, California.

Visit some of his websites
http://www.AddMeInNow.com
http://www.AppliedMindSciences.com
http://www.BookbuilderPLUS.com
http://www.BookJumping.com
http://www.EmailNations.com
http://www.EmbarrassingProblemsFix.com
http://www.ePubWealth.com
http://www.ForensicsNation.com
http://www.ForensicsNationStore.com
http://www.FreebiesNation.com
http://www.HealthFitnessWellnessNation.com
http://www.Neternatives.com

http://www.PrivacyNations.com
http://www.RetireWithoutMoney.org
http://www.SurvivalNations.com
http://www.TheBentonKitchen.com
http://www.Theolegions.org
http://www.VideoBookbuilder.com

Some Other Books You May Enjoy From ePubWealth.com, LLC Library Catalog

EPW Library Catalog Online
http://www.epubwealth.com/wp-content/uploads/2013/07/Leland-benton-private-turbo.pdf

EPW Library Catalog Download
http://www.filefactory.com/f/562ef3ea1a054f0a